HOW TO PLAY
THE RECORDER

A Beginner's Guide to Learn to
Play the Recorder with Follow
Along Audio Examples

Table of Contents

Throughout this book there are musical examples and audio recordings to follow along with on your journey to learn how to play the recorder.

Whenever you see the following words:

Play: [Followed By the Title of the Recording]

Please follow along with the recordings at the Sound Cloud link below or search on Sound Cloud for "How to Play the Recorder".

https://soundcloud.com/jason_randall/sets/how-to-play-the-recorder

Introduction

Hello and welcome to *Let's Play the Recorder*! Here you will learn technique, history, and fundamentals of recorder performance. Over the years, this flutophone has garnered a reputation of being a child's instrument because of its ease of play and teachability, but in the right hands it can be a formidable tool of musical sound, just like any other instrument. Be prepared to have fun and be challenged, as there is a wide array of skills to discover. Good luck and enjoy the journey!

History of the Recorder

The earliest members of duct flutes (the class of flutes that are closest to recorders) date to the Neolithic, or New Stone Age, close to 10,000 years ago. Instruments of this class are found in almost every musical tradition in the world. The distinguishing trait of the recorder is its thumbhole, which is used to change the register of produced pitches.

The Renaissance period (14th-17th century) was the first time performance practice, structure, and repertoire of the recorder were documented. As such, a large portion of the instrument's musical library comes from this period. Later classical periods (late Baroque-20th Century) seldom used the recorder because of its limited dynamic, timbral, and tonal range compared to the modern flute.

About the Recorder

The recorder is an internal duct flute (a flute with a whistle mouthpiece) that is part of the woodwind family. It is distinguishable from other duct flutes by the presence of a thumbhole on the bottom and seven finger holes on top. The last two finger holes contain partitions used to produce chromatic pitches (pitches making up the smallest distance of space able to be musically notated). There is a *D/D♯* chromatic partition on the sixth and a *C/C♯* on the seventh. The octave above the base set of notes can be accessed by two means: half-holing the thumbhole or overblowing. Other chromatic pitches can be produced by half-holing or covering the two holes that skip the note hole preceding the targeted pitch. This system of pitch production is not as elegant as its modern woodwind cousins, but a skilled recorder player can circumvent these challenges by producing scales and techniques that reproduce the effects of instruments such as the flute, clarinet, and bassoon.

The Recorder Family

The recorder family is vast. With its cousins, aunties, uncles, nephews, grandchildren, great-grandchildren, and anyone else you can think of, there is a wide array of variants covering the spectrum of musical pitch. The most common recorder used is the soprano, which is pitched in the key of *C* (more on that later). This *C*-soprano's small size, moderate range, intonation, and ease of play make it ideal as the introductory member of its unit. There are over eight types of recorder, but we will focus on the main three.

Soprano Recorder

This is the most common type of recorder and is pitched in the key of *C*. The notes of this instrument sound an octave higher than written, matching the written pitches of instruments such as the piccolo. The lowest note is *C* and the highest varies depending on the instrument and skill of the player.

Alto Recorder

The alto is the second most common, pitched in the key of *F*. The notes of this instrument sound a fourth (or four diatonic notes) higher than written. The lowest note is *C* (sounds *F*) and the highest varies depending on the instrument and skill of the player. Any time an instrument is pitched in a key, that key determines the pitch that is produced when the performer plays its *C*, hence why an instrument in *F* sounds *F* when the player fingers a *C*. The graph shows an antiquated style of writing for the alto, however the pitch range remains the same (notice the lowest note is *F*).

Tenor Recorder

This is the third most common, pitched in the key of *C*. The notes of this instrument sound exactly as written. This is the only member of the family that matches its notated pitch. The lowest note is *C* and the highest varies depending on the instrument and skill of the player.

The Numbers of Music

Western music has a vocabulary of twelve distinct pitches per octave. You can think of it like this: There are only ten numbers in the standard occidental count, but depending on how they are combined, they can create virtually limitless permutations. 0, 1, 2, 3, 4, 5, 6, 7, 8, and 9 are the only numerical characters, but by placing a 1, 2, or any other number (besides 0) in front of another, we can go outside of the original set. This is where octaves come in. The same way that 0, 1, 2, and 3 can become 10, 11, 12, and 13, the notes *A*, *B*, *C*, and so on can become higher *A*'s, *B*'s, and *C*'s by changing the octave. An octave is changed visually by placing a note higher or lower on a staff. Because there are only twelve pitches, anytime a note is placed outside of a certain set, it is then in a new octave, the same way that once a certain numerical threshold is passed, a new set is entered.

Numerical sets are named ones (0-9), tens (10-99), hundreds (100-999), etc. Pitch sets are numbered octaves, where the first octave (typically the lowest possible on the deepest instruments) is appropriately labeled 0. Because **C** is diatonically the most neutral key, the octave classes revolve around it the same way numerical sets are centered around one. C1, C2, and C3 are analogous to 1, 10, and 100, respectively.

Time Signature and Beats

A time signature is the indication of a beat source. There are two parts to a time signature: an upper number and a lower number. The upper number represents how many beats or pulses are in a measure and the lower number defines what the beat is. If 4 is in the lower number, that means the beat belongs to the quarter note. If 2, then the half note. If 1 (this is rare), then the whole note. If 8 was the lower number, what would get the pulse? If you guessed the eighth note, you are correct! 4/4 time is the most common (fittingly known as "common time") and will be used for most of the upcoming exercises. Here is a chart detailing the note lengths with respect to one another and a breakdown of a few common time signatures and what they mean:

(Credit to musiceducationwhiz.com)

Measures and Barlines

Measures are the areas occupying the spaces between two barlines. They contain the total number of suggested beats determined by the time signature (save for special situations like cadenzas or improvisation). Barlines are lines that are used to divide measures (for ease of reading and organization of music). The image shows what measures and barlines look like:

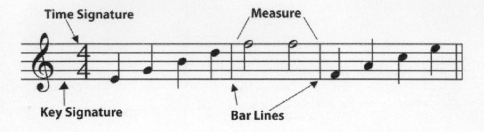

Clefs

The clef is the symbol at the beginning or middle of a selection that expresses the location of a certain pitch on the staff. All other pitches are organized from the pitch designated. Because this manual is for playing the recorder, we will only review the treble clef.

The treble clef is the symbol on a staff (five horizontal lines with four horizontal spaces) that designates the location of *G*. From here, we can determine the location of all other pitches. Using mnemonic devices, we can remember the locations of each note by reciting "*E*very *G*ood *B*oy *D*oes *F*ine on the line" and "*FACE* in the space."

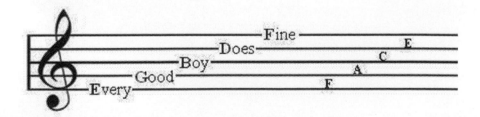

How to Play the Recorder

The Mouth

The embouchure for the recorder should be relaxed, with the lips creating a seal on the mouthpiece of the instrument. Although the tongue is used for accentation and annunciation of notes, it should be at rest for a neutral tone. Air blown into the recorder should be hardly more forceful than breathing, as overblowing will send the instrument into its upper octaves with unstable, out of tune, and shrill pitches.

The Fingers

The left hand should be placed closest to the mouthpiece, taking up the thumbhole and the top first three finger holes, while the pinky rests along the side of the instrument, stabilizing it. The right hand uses the thumb to support the underside of the instrument while the index, middle, ring, and pinky fingers cover the remaining holes.

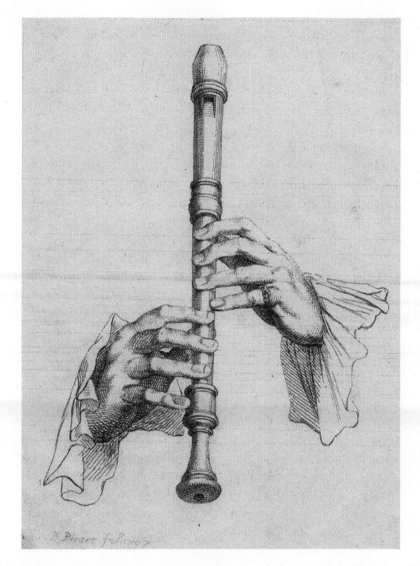

Note Values

We're almost ready to play! But before we do, we must cover note values. Note values are the lengths of time each note is to be played and each value is shown by a unique symbol. Study the chart to learn the symbols and how their values relate to one another. The chart also includes rests (periods when you do not play), so feel free to learn how they relate as well. No pressure, though, as we will cover them in the future. For now, all you need to know are note lengths and how they're written.

NOTE & REST CHART

Name	Note	Rest	Beats	1 $\frac{4}{4}$ measure
Whole	𝅝	▬	4	𝅝
Half	𝅗𝅥	▬	2	𝅗𝅥 𝅗𝅥
Quarter	♩	𝄽	1	♩ ♩ ♩ ♩
Eighth	♪	𝄾	½	♫ ♫ ♫ ♫
Sixteenth	𝅘𝅥𝅯	𝄿	¼	𝅘𝅥𝅲𝅘𝅥𝅲𝅘𝅥𝅲𝅘𝅥𝅲 𝅘𝅥𝅲𝅘𝅥𝅲𝅘𝅥𝅲𝅘𝅥𝅲 𝅘𝅥𝅲𝅘𝅥𝅲𝅘𝅥𝅲𝅘𝅥𝅲 𝅘𝅥𝅲𝅘𝅥𝅲𝅘𝅥𝅲𝅘𝅥𝅲

The Pitches

G is the first pitch we will review. Listen to what it sounds like

Play: 01 Recorder G1

G is located on the second line of the treble clef staff. Because of the location of the note on the instrument (in the middle), it is relatively easy to produce with little to no risk of overblowing. To finger the note, place the left thumb over the thumbhole and cover the first three holes with the same hand. Once you've done that, try performing the rhythm notated below. There will be a click track that plays along to help you keep in time with the rhythm (links shown at the bottom as "Ex."). It will give you four preparatory beats so you can internalize the tempo, and then you can begin. It may be best to listen first and practice counting the beat as you read the music.

1. **Play: 02 Recorder Exercise G1**

2. **Play: 03 Recorder Exercise G2**
3. **Play: 04 Recorder Exercise G3**
4. **Play: 05 Recorder Exercise G4**

A is the second pitch we will learn. It is one diatonic step higher than *G*, located in the second space of the treble clef staff. Here we cover one less finger hole, utilizing the thumbhole and the first two openings above. There are rhythmic examples for you to try below. You will alternate between *G* and *A* in all but one.

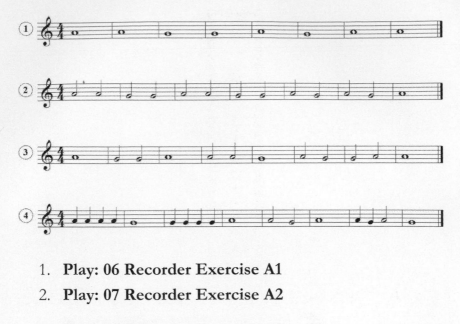

1. **Play: 06 Recorder Exercise A1**
2. **Play: 07 Recorder Exercise A2**

3. **Play: 08 Recorder Exercise A3**

4. **Play: 09 Recorder Exercise A4**

B is the third pitch in our expanding musical vocabulary. It is one diatonic step higher than *A* and a major third interval higher than *G*. It is located on the third line of the treble clef staff. Try the rhythms below, noting the difference between *B* and *G* and taking care of the jumps between them.

1. **Play: 10 Recorder Exercise B1**

2. **Play: 11 Recorder Exercise B2**

3. **Play: 12 Recorder Exercise B3**
4. **Play: 13 Recorder Exercise B4**

5. **Play: 14 Recorder Exercise B5**

C is the next pitch we'll discover. This one is a semitone higher than the last (*B*). Unlike prior notes, the semitone between them means *B* and *C* are a half step away from one another, whereas the others are a whole step or more. To perform it, the left thumb will cover the thumbhole while the middle finger covers the second finger hole, skipping the index finger. There are a number of exercises to practice below:

1. **Play: 15 Recorder Exercise C1**

2. **Play: 16 Recorder Exercise C2**

3. **Play: 17 Recorder Exercise C3**

4. **Play: 18 Recorder Exercise C4**

5. **Play: 19 Recorder Exercise C5**

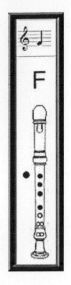

Having reached our **C**, we will now head in the opposite direction, to go below our first learned pitch, **G**, to **F**. **F** is a whole tone lower than **G** and will require the use of both hands. To execute it, cover the thumbhole and first three finger holes with the left hand while covering the fourth and sixth thumbholes with the right hand, skipping the middle finger. With **F** in your pitch vocabulary, you can now play more than one half of a scale. Congratulations! Attempt the exercises below to review all the notes you've learned up to this point. Be wary of the arpeggios in the fifth exercise. If you're feeling confident, try the challenge excerpt!

1. **Play: 20 Recorder Exercise F1**

2. **Play: 21 Recorder Exercise F2**

3. **Play: 22 Recorder Exercise F3**

4. **Play: 23 Recorder Exercise F4**

5. **Play: 24 Recorder Exercise F5**

"Mary Had A Little Lamb"

Challenge!

Play: 25 Recorder Exercise Mary

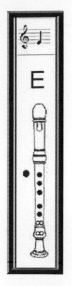

We will continue moving downward to our next pitch, *E*. *E* is one half step (semitone) below *F*. As such, there is no chromatic tone between them (more on chromaticism later). To execute the note, cover the thumbhole and the first five finger holes consecutively without skips. Attempt the passages below to improve dexterity:

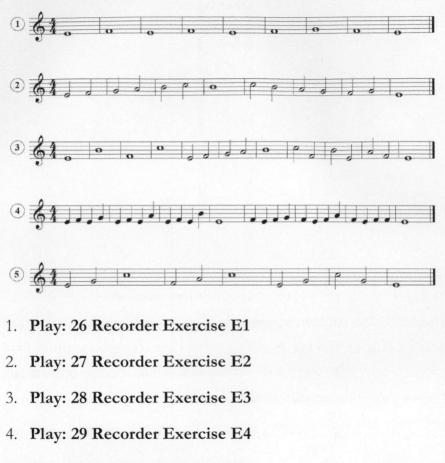

1. **Play: 26 Recorder Exercise E1**

2. **Play: 27 Recorder Exercise E2**

3. **Play: 28 Recorder Exercise E3**

4. **Play: 29 Recorder Exercise E4**

5. **Play: 30 Recorder Exercise E5**

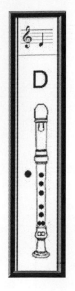

The next pitch we'll learn is **D**. **D** is a whole step lower than **E**. To obtain the pitch, cover the thumbhole and the first six finger holes. Now we're just one step away from completing our first octave and scale! Practice the samples below to master movement between the hands. As always, watch out for the interval jumps!

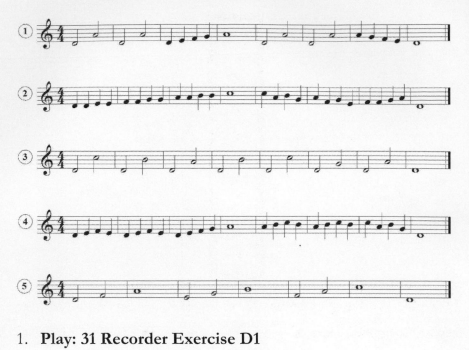

1. **Play: 31 Recorder Exercise D1**

2. **Play: 32 Recorder Exercise D2**

3. **Play: 33 Recorder Exercise D3**

4. **Play: 34 Recorder Exercise D4**

5. **Play: 35 Recorder Exercise D5**

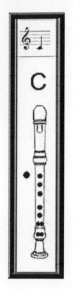

Hazzah! You've finally made it to the lowest note on the recorder: low *C*. Low *C* is an octave below the higher middle *C* we encountered earlier. Low *C* is also a whole tone below *D*. To execute it, cover all holes of the instrument. Try the examples below, the most difficult tests so far. If you have trouble, do not give up!

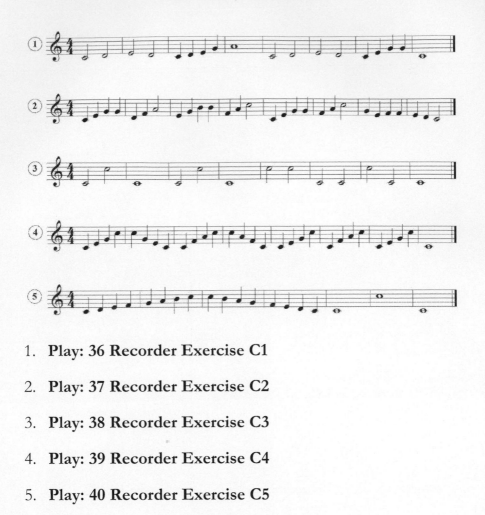

1. **Play: 36 Recorder Exercise C1**

2. **Play: 37 Recorder Exercise C2**

3. **Play: 38 Recorder Exercise C3**

4. **Play: 39 Recorder Exercise C4**

5. **Play: 40 Recorder Exercise C5**

Twinkle, Twinkle

Challenge!

Play: 41 Recorder Exercise C6 Twinkle

The Pitches

Congratulations on completing your first octave! Now it's time to explore the second octave of the recorder. As you are now more comfortable on the instrument, we will go over each new pitch more quickly.

Middle **D** is the next note we'll learn. It is a whole step above middle **D** and an octave above the first low **D** we learned. To perform it place your middle finger on the second finger hole, leaving the first and thumbhole uncovered. Attempt the examples below to further expand your range. You'll notice a *fermata* in one of the examples. A fermata is used to signal that you are to hold a note longer than it is written.

1. **Play: 42 Recorder Exercise D1**

2. **Play: 43 Recorder Exercise D2**

3. **Play: 44 Recorder Exercise D3**

4. **Play: 45 Recorder Exercise D4**
5. **Play: 46 Recorder Exercise D5**

Next is middle *E*. This is a step above our previously learned middle *D*. To execute it, we need to employ a new technique known as "half-holing." Half-holing allows you to access the upper range of the instrument while staying in tune. More specifically, half-holing transposes most pitches in the lower range of the recorder up an octave, like adding a "0" at the end of a number to send it into the next numerical set (ex: 10 to 100). To half-hole, you cover only part of the thumbhole. Just like before with the low *E*, you're going to place your finger over the first five finger holes on top but cover only the thumbhole halfway. The exercises below will challenge you to utilize both standard and half-hole techniques. Notice the dot marks next to the half notes in one of the examples. A dot means to hold the note for its full value plus half. So, a half note with a dot gets three beats instead of two. Also notice the *ritards* (*rit.*). Anytime you see this, you should gradually slow down. These are usually placed at the end of a piece to make it sound smoother. Good luck and keep at it!

1. **Play: 47 Recorder Exercise E1**

2. **Play: 48 Recorder Exercise E2**

3. **Play: 49 Recorder Exercise E3**
4. **Play: 50 Recorder Exercise E4**

5. **Play: 51 Recorder Exercise E5**

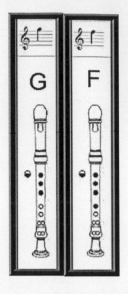

We will now move on to high **F** and **G**. To perform **F**, half-hole the thumb position and cover the first six holes, skipping the fifth. To perform **G**, half-hole the thumb position and cover the first three holes. Try the exercises below to explore the higher register of your instrument. Be aware of the dotted quarter notes; they are one and a half beats long. The eighth notes that follow are half a beat long. That means, in total, a dotted quarter and eighth will occupy two beats.

1. **Play: 52 Recorder Exercise FG1**

2. **Play: 53 Recorder Exercise FG2**

3. **Play: 54 Recorder Exercise FG3**

4. **Play: 55 Recorder Exercise FG4**

5. **Play: 56 Recorder Exercise FG5**

The Chromatic Pitches

Now that we've explored the upper octave, it's time to cork the nooks and crannies of the pitches we've learned thus far. These nooks and crannies are known as chromaticism. Chromaticism refers to the semitones between the natural notes we've learned. Non-natural notes are notated with either the flat or sharp symbol. Sharps raise a pitch by a half step (semitone), flats lower by the same, and a natural cancels the other two out. Remember, a semitone is one half of a whole tone, and you'll recall the only pairs of natural notes that are a semitone apart are *E/F* and *B/C*. Look at the image; you can see that there is nothing in between them. Now try alternating among the notes *B* and *C*, then *A* and *B* to see if you can hear the difference.

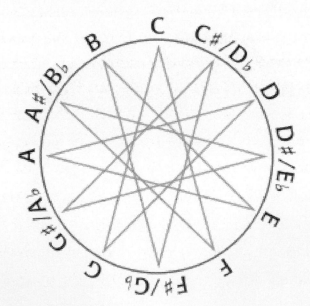

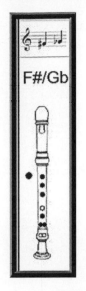

The first chromatic tone we'll tackle is *F♯*. (For the sake of simplicity, ignore the enharmonic spelling; we will cover equivalents later.) Again, we call the symbol ♯ a sharp. So, *F♯* is vocalized as "F-sharp." To play it, cover the thumbhole and the first six finger holes, skipping the fourth. Try the exercises below to begin your mastery of chromaticism and pay attention to how sharps and naturals interact with one another. Notice that anytime a non-diatonic pitch is introduced (one that does not fit the key signature), this pitch is canceled by the barline. So, if you have no sharps or flats in the key signature but encounter an *F♯*, that *F♯* will turn back to *F♮* (F natural) in the next measure. The opposite is also true. Pay attention to the key signature of the first and second exercises. The sharp sign on the second exercise is on the *F* line, so that means all *F*'s are to be played sharp, unless a flat or natural is introduced.

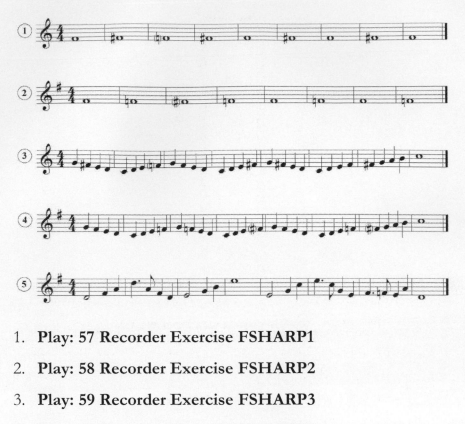

1. **Play: 57 Recorder Exercise FSHARP1**

2. **Play: 58 Recorder Exercise FSHARP2**

3. **Play: 59 Recorder Exercise FSHARP3**

4. **Play: 60 Recorder Exercise FSHARP4**

5. **Play: 61 Recorder Exercise FSHARP5**

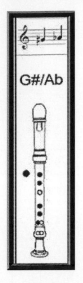

G♯ is our next chromatic pitch. To execute it, cover the thumbhole and the first five finger holes, leaving the third open (you do not have to cover one of the double holes in the sixth position, except for tuning purposes). The exercises below will challenge you to use multiple chromatic pitches. Pay attention to the eighth notes here; there are two of them per beat.

1. **Play: 62 Recorder Exercise GSHARP1**

2. **Play: 63 Recorder Exercise GSHARP2**

3. **Play: 64 Recorder Exercise GSHARP3**
4. **Play: 65 Recorder Exercise GSHARP4**

5. **Play: 66 Recorder Exercise GSHARP5**

We'll move onto *B*♭ now. Remember the ♭ symbol is called a flat, so *B*♭ is vocalized as "B flat." It is a semitone higher than *A* and a whole tone lower than *C*. To play it, cover the thumbhole and first four finger holes, skipping the second. Perform the exercises below to expand your chromatic vocabulary. Take care of the dotted eighth notes. They get ¾ of a beat. You can subdivide each beat into four parts with the syllables "1" "e" "and" "a" (the "1" can be replaced by whatever beat is being subdivided. So, beat 3 would be subdivided as "3" "e" "and" "a"). A dotted eighth on the first beat would get "1" "e" "and" and the sixteenth that follows would get the "a". Good luck!

1. **Play: 67 Recorder Exercise BFlat1**

2. **Play: 68 Recorder Exercise BFlat2**

3. **Play: 69 Recorder Exercise BFlat3**

4. **Play: 70 Recorder Exercise BFlat4**

5. **Play: 71 Recorder Exercise BFlat5**

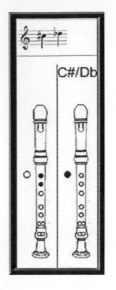

Onto middle **C♯**. This is the easiest note to play; all you need to do is cover the thumbhole. We will also introduce a new ¾ time signature. Now instead of each measure getting four pulses, each gets three. That means there can be no whole notes. Have fun!

1. **Play: 72 Recorder Exercise CSharp1**
2. **Play: 73 Recorder Exercise CSharp2**
3. **Play: 74 Recorder Exercise CSharp3**
4. **Play: 75 Recorder Exercise CSharp4**
5. **Play: 76 Recorder Exercise CSharp5**

"Greensleeves" is a popular Christmas piece about the love of a king for a woman who wore - you guessed it - green sleeves. Note that the piece is in ¾ time. Not a problem, as you have already played exercises in that time signature. Also, if you're wondering what those tiny numbers in the top left corners of the measures are, they are known as "measure numbers." Not everything in life must be complicated! These measure numbers help you keep track of where you are in longer pieces of music. Lastly, in the very beginning of the piece is an incomplete measure known as a "pickup measure." These are used when an entire measure is not needed to begin a piece.

Greensleeves

Challenge

Play: 77 Recorder Exercise CSharp6 Greensleeves

Rests

Before we continue expanding our chromatic knowledge of the recorder, we will focus on the concept of rests. Rests are notations in music signifying a break in play. They are like waiting at a red light; once their time has passed, you can continue. There are many kinds of rests, but we will cover only the major five. Note that dots can apply to rests as well, so a dotted quarter rest in common time gets a beat and a half long break. Below are the most common ones you'll encounter:

Whole Rest (▬): A musical break lasting an entire measure. (Not necessarily the length of a whole note, especially if the measure is longer than four beats.) Distinguished from a half rest because it hangs downward.

Half Rest (▬): A musical break lasting the length of a half note. Distinguished from a whole rest because it sits upright.

Quarter Rest (𝄽): A musical break lasting the length of a quarter note.

Eighth Rest (𝄾): A musical break lasting the length of an eighth note.

Sixteenth Rest (𝄿): A musical break lasting the length of a sixteenth note.

Many of the upcoming exercises will begin featuring rests now. Refer to the audio recordings for help if you need it.

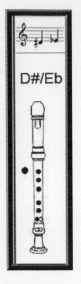

Low *E*b is the next pitch we'll learn. This will be the first time we'll fully utilize those strange looking two-part holes at the end of the instrument. To perform it, cover the thumbhole and the first five finger holes. Once you get to the sixth hole at the end of the instrument, cover only the larger of the two holes, leaving the second set of holes open. Try the practices below and make sure to pause during the rests:

1. **Play: 78 Recorder Exercise EFlat1**

2. **Play: 79 Recorder Exercise EFlat2**

3. **Play: 80 Recorder Exercise EFlat3**

4. **Play: 81 Recorder Exercise EFlat4**

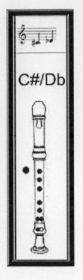

Next is low *C♯*. Just like *E*♭, you will cover one of holes from the odd-looking pair. To execute it, cover the thumbhole, the first six finger holes (including both holes in the sixth position), and only the larger of the two holes in the seventh and last position. Perform the exercises below taking note of how exercise 3 covers more than one line (just like in "Greensleeves"). Also, pay attention to the A♯ in the third measure of example 2. An A♯ is equivalent to a B♭; this equivalence is known as enharmonicism. We will cover enharmonicism more thoroughly in a later section.

1. **Play: 82 Recorder Exercise CSharp1**

2. **Play: 83 Recorder Exercise CSharp2**

3. **Play: 84 Recorder Exercise CSharp3**

Middle *E*b is our next note. To play it, cover half of the thumbhole, the first five finger holes, and the large segment of the sixth position, just like with the low *E*b (save the thumbhole). You're almost done with the two main octaves of the recorder! Take note of the similarities between these exercises and the previous ones. What is the same and what is different?

1. **Play: 85 Recorder Exercise EFlat1**

2. **Play: 86 Recorder Exercise EFlat2**

3. **Play: 87 Recorder Exercise EFlat3**

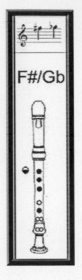

Onto *F♯*. To play this higher chromatic pitch, the thumbhole is half covered while the first five finger holes are covered, skipping the fourth position. The exercises below will test your ability to switch octaves and will be the hardest test of your skills yet. You will also notice strange-looking smaller notes in front of the regularly-sized pitches. These are grace notes, which are to be played on or before the beat depending on whether they are slashed. The slashed notes are to be played right before the downbeat and the un-slashed notes are to be played on the downbeat. Lastly, there is an *accel.* marking in exercise 3. This means to speed up until you reach the end of the dotted line. I've said it a few times before, but this time I mean it - good luck!

1. **Play: 88 Recorder Exercise FSharp1**
2. **Play: 89 Recorder Exercise FSharp2**

3. **Play: 90 Recorder Exercise FSharp3**
4. **Play: 91 Recorder Exercise FSharp4**

Enharmonicism

Enharmonicism is the alternate spelling for notes that are identical. An example of enharmonic notes are **C♯** and **D♭, where the sharp raises the** *C* and the flat lowers the *D*. You can think of it as 3 equaling 2+1 or 4-1, where the +1 is the sharp and the -1 is the flat. There is only one whole number between 2 and 4, so approaching it from above or below gives the same result. The only time this is untrue is between the notes *B* and *C* and *E* and *F*, because there is no pitch between them. As such, a *B♯* would be a *C*, a *C♭* a *B*, an *E♯* an *F*, and an *F♭* an *E*. Review the chart and explore enharmonicism in the examples below:

Enharmonic Equivalent Notes

C♯ = D♭

D♯ = E♭

E♯ = F

E = F♭

F♯ = G♭

G♯ = A♭

A♯ = B♭

B♯ = C

B = C♭

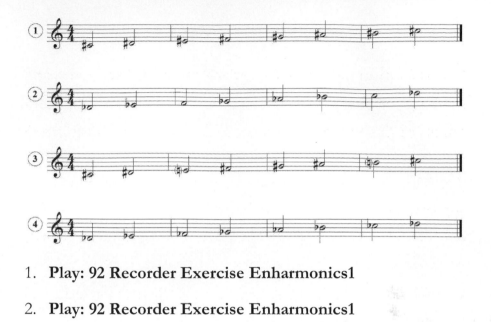

1. **Play: 92 Recorder Exercise Enharmonics1**

2. **Play: 92 Recorder Exercise Enharmonics1**

3. **Play: 93 Recorder Exercise Enharmonics34**

4. **Play: 93 Recorder Exercise Enharmonics34**

Extended Techniques

Well done on completing the fundamentals of the recorder! From now on, we will focus on extended techniques. These include the expansion of range, articulation, dynamics, and compound time. The recorder is a marvelous instrument and we hope that reading this guide will encourage you to continue playing. Now, onto more!

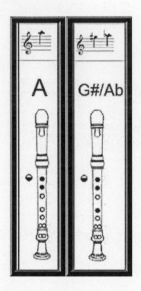

High *G♯/A*b is performed by half-holing the thumb position and covering the first four finger holes, skipping the third. High *A* is executed by half-holing the thumbhole and covering the first two finger holes. The notes in this range of the instrument are far more unstable than the others and you're likely to squeak. With practice, you'll find the right balance of embouchure and airflow to stabilize the pitches. Try the exercises below to further advance your play. You'll see the *"accel."* marking; this lasts through to the "*a tempo*," where you continue at the original speed.

1. **Play: 94 Recorder Exercise GSHARPA1**

2. **Play: 95 Recorder Exercise GSHARPA2**

3. **Play: 96 Recorder Exercise GSHARPA3**

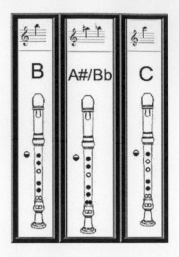

High **B**♭, **B**, and double high **C** are the next pitches in the upper register of the recorder. The notes up here require a technique known as "overblowing." Overblowing requires you to channel a more forceful stream of air through the instrument to achieve the higher notes. It's likely that when you first began, you overblew pitches that sounded like squeaks. In reality, those squeaks were just out-of-control, unintentional pitches. To play the new notes, half-hole the thumb position, then cover the first two finger holes, skipping the third. Cover the fourth, fifth, and sixth for the **B**♭, releasing the sixth, but keep the rest the same for the **B**. Release the second finger hole while covering the fourth and fifth for the **C**. Try the examples below to improve your skills with these stratospheric pitches:

1. **Play: 97 Recorder Exercise BFlatBC1**
2. **Play: 98 Recorder Exercise BFlatBC2**

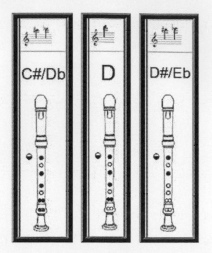

Double high C♯/D♭, D, and E♭/D♯ are the last notes we'll learn. They are shrill, exceptionally difficult to play, and impractical in most musical situations. However, don't let that stop you from trying them! To perform C♯, half-hole the thumb position and cover the first, third, fourth, sixth, and seventh finger holes. It is important to overblow to produce the correct pitch by accessing the higher harmonic. (For reference, a harmonic or the harmonic series of a pitch is akin to the light spectrum of a color. The color of light you see isn't the only color of light in its makeup, but instead a wide array of wavelengths of color. What you see is the dominant wavelength being reflected. It's the same with pitch; the sound you hear is the dominant frequency of a wide array of harmonic sounds. If you listen to an organ play one note or a bell ring in a cathedral, you'll notice there's more than one sound.) To perform D, release the seventh position, keeping airflow high. Finally, to achieve the hardest note, E♭, release the fourth and sixth positions. Try the examples below to test your overblowing technique:

1. **Play: 99 Recorder Exercise DFlatDEFlat12**
2. **Play: 99 Recorder Exercise DFlatDEFlat12**

Dynamics

Dynamics are instructions on how loud or soft to play music. Below is a chart detailing them:

Term:	Symbol:	Effect:
piano	p	soft
pianissimo	pp	very soft
mezzo piano	mp	slightly soft
forte	f	loud
fortissimo	ff	very loud
mezzo forte	mf	slightly loud
fortepiano	fp	loud then soft
sforzando	sfz	sudden accent
crescendo	$<$	gradually louder
diminuendo	$>$	gradually softer

Try the exercises below that utilize these dynamics:

68

1. **Play: 100 Recorder Exercise Dynamics1**
2. **Play: 101 Recorder Exercise Dynamics2**

Ties

Ties are curved lines used to combine the lengths of notes, particularly in situations when there isn't enough time allotted in a measure. Perform the examples below to practice ties:

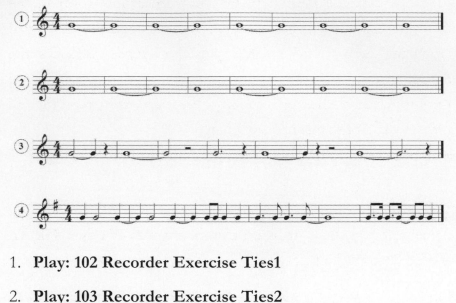

1. **Play: 102 Recorder Exercise Ties1**

2. **Play: 103 Recorder Exercise Ties2**

3. **Play: 104 Recorder Exercise Ties3**

4. **Play: 105 Recorder Exercise Ties4**

Articulations

Articulations are the manner in which notes are attacked. There are a wide variety of expressions, so we'll focus on the major ones. In general, when there is no articulation, you are expected to gently separate each note by stopping airflow through the instrument gently with your tongue. This technique is aptly called "tonguing" and a "ta" syllable with the tongue produces the desired effect. Try tonguing exercises from now on to get a feel for the difference in tone quality. You may even want to visit previous sections and apply tonguing there.

Accent

An accent suggests a stress on a note or group of notes. Play an accented note slightly louder than non-accented notes.

Staccato

Notes with the staccato marking should be played shorter than notes without the marking.

Marcato

A combination of staccato and accent, marcato suggests playing a note slightly louder and shorter than non-marcato notes.

Legato/Tenuto

The opposite of staccato, legato notes are held as long as possible between tonguing.

Slur

Similar in sound to legato, slurring suggests no tonguing between notes and that all notes are played with continuous sound.

Trill

A trill is a rapid alternation between two pitches next to one another. Usually the diatonic pitch just above the written note is what is trilled to.

Tremolo

Like a trill, a tremolo connects pitches further away from one another than a diatonic pitch just above, the trill's bigger sister. The note values are not added. So, a tremolo with two whole notes is played for the length of one whole note. Likewise with all other note lengths.

Turn

Usually following a trill, a turn is a quick succession of notes that are played, often starting with the base pitch (the one written), then to the diatonic right above, back to the original pitch, then to the diatonic below, and finally back to the original. Turns are most common in Baroque music.

Flutter

Flutter tonguing is a stuttering or fluttering sound that is created by rolling or vibrating the tongue while blowing into your instrument. It should almost sound like you are playing your recorder near a fan.

Glissando

A glissando is a rapid succession of notes played from the bottom written pitch to the top. It should sound like running your hands up the keys of a piano.

Try the exercises below, which will require some of the accents. What is different about the two pieces? The same? Which do you prefer?

1. **Play: 106 Recorder Exercise Articulations12**

2. **Play: 106 Recorder Exercise Articulations12**

Triplets, Compound Time, and Cut Time

So far we've only dealt with duple (common) time, time and note values divisible by two and four. Now we will discuss triple (compound) time. Compound time is a meter of music that is divisible by three. There are meters of music that are divisible by other numbers, but those are irregular and we will not cover them here. In a compound meter, you'll often see the number 8 in the bottom position of a time signature, which you'll recall means that the eighth note gets the beat. This is done for simplification purposes, to count and divide rhythms that would otherwise be cumbersome with longer pulses (counting three eighth notes is easier than trying to divide a quarter note into three equal pieces). For reference, here is the time signature chart again, showing the number of beats in each measure of time signature:

www.musiceducationwhiz.com

75

Triplets

Triplets are a subset of compound time, which means they have the feel of a triple meter, but can be played in a common time piece. The opposite also holds true; duple rhythms can be played in triple meter. Triplets are notated with the number 3 above a group of notes (usually bracketed), signaling that the beat is to be divided into three equal parts.

Cut Time

Cut time is a variation of common duple meter time, but instead of the quarter note getting the beat, the half note does. In essence, cut time is twice as fast as common time. It is indicated by a C with a vertical line through its center (also known as a cent sign) or as a 2 over 2 equation. The exercises below will cover all three previously mentioned variations of time. (Please note that the beat is for a quarter, dotted quarter, and half, respectively.)

1. **Play: 107 Recorder Exercise Time Signature123**

2. **Play: 107 Recorder Exercise Time Signature123**

3. **Play: 107 Recorder Exercise Time Signature123**

Tempo Marks

Almost all the recordings for the exercises have been performed at a pulse of about 90 beats per second. However, not all music has the same speed. This is where tempo marks come in. They can be written as general suggestions (Allegro, Largo, Fast, Slow), specific measures of time ($\quarternote=120$), or both. As you begin to explore the repertoire of the recorder outside this manual, you will encounter such markings. The challenges below will be your final obstacles. They are extremely difficult and will test your abilities to their limits. Do not become frustrated if you cannot perform them yet; we assume that you have taken years to get this far in the manual. If you have just started, master the previous exercises and come back later.

TEMPO MARKINGS

Larghissimo — very, very slow (20 bpm and below)

Grave — slow and solemn (20–40 bpm)

Lento — slowly (40–60 bpm)

Largo — broadly (40–60 bpm)
Larghetto — rather broadly (60–66 bpm)

Adagio — slow and stately (literally, "at ease") (66–76 bpm)
Adagietto — rather slow (70–80 bpm)
Andante moderato — a bit slower than andante

Andante — at a walking pace (76–108 bpm)
Andantino – slightly faster than andante

Moderato — moderately (108–120 bpm)
Allegretto — moderately fast (but less so than allegro)
Allegro moderato — moderately quick (112–124 bpm)

Allegro — fast, quickly and bright (120–168 bpm)

Vivace — lively and fast (≈140 bpm) (quicker than allegro)
Vivacissimo — very fast and lively
Allegrissimo — very fast

Presto — very fast (168–200 bpm)
Prestissimo — extremely fast (more than 200bpm)

Ritardando

Accelerando

79

The Final Challenges

As previously said, these final challenges are extremely difficult. They are all excerpts from famous pieces that were written for other instruments. You will see the familiar "Play!" button that will allow you to hear the part and the "Performance!" button that will execute the excerpt in the piece for which it was written. Good luck and have fun!

"The Grand Duel"
AKA: Oren-Ishii from, "Kill Bill"

Sergio Bardotti

Play: 108 The Grand Duel

Performance!

https://drive.google.com/open?id=1DobBXyiKoP5EJXbtOXA IghcAIcxbjikw

Barber of Seville
Overture

G. Rossini

Play: 110 Barber of Seville

Performance!

Play: 111 Barber of Seville Audio

Night On Bald Mountain
Clarinet and Flute Solos

M. Mussorgsky

Play: 112 Night On Bald Mountain

Performance!

https://drive.google.com/open?id=1W2aNpU9pfoxXpKnZtAv
Fmk7nNH-A3XKy

Play: 114 Fur Elise

Performance!

https://drive.google.com/open?id=10a8ZHygM60Zwi5xASXry
Unw8GzXF_zeu

Swan Lake

Main Theme

P. I. Tchaikovsky

Play: 116 Swan Lake

Performance!

https://drive.google.com/open?id=1fcV0Soja9NIYzY5siGhVZr_m5HY_Eevy

Marche Slav
Main Theme

P. I. Tchaikovsky

Play:

https://drive.google.com/open?id=1FQhajKes4nuXvDfbyFfEi
mRBIRBanIAF

Performance!

https://drive.google.com/open?id=1-
TAjpeZfyFPpY1RJ6ovwi04Og98slJyO

Stars And Stripes Forever

Piccolo Solo

J. P. Sousa

Play:

https://drive.google.com/open?id=1nlwDNEZfJXkE7LV9IMT
96L62Kt8B3CRZ

Performance!

https://drive.google.com/open?id=1I4RnHz50rKQVSaH0CKC
KAiUNHoMLJlcb

The Sorcerer's Apprentice
Main Theme

P. Dukas

Play:

https://drive.google.com/open?id=19qJHXsdlUbrYXIdZbbk9p
U7W6LG2xK7U

Performance!

https://drive.google.com/open?id=1Rl2BGK7RH7DGKURmd
rHo9HTriZlWIRqT

Glossary of Terms

8ᵛᵃ : Play an octave higher than written.

Accent: An articulation suggesting that the marked note be stressed or played louder than unmarked notes.

Arpeggio: The playing of notes of a chord up or down, individually, and usually in rapid succession.

Articulation: Musical marking indicating the manner in which a note is to be played.

Barline: The line(s) used to separate measures.

Bar Repeat: A blocked out and notated measure used to indicate the repetition of (a) previous measure(s).

Beat: The pulse of a performed piece of music. Each pulse corresponds directly to the tempo assigned.

Chord: A group of three or more notes played at the same time.

Chromaticism: The division of intervals into their smallest values.

Clef: The symbol placed at the beginning or middle of a piece signifying the location of a specific note on which all other notes are based. For example, the treble clef (also known as the G-clef) shows where the *G* is on its staff. A bass clef (also known as the F-clef) shows where the *F* is.

Compound Time: The musical rhythm or meter in which each beat in a bar is subdivided (broken down) into three smaller units or parts.

Cut Time: A duple meter that uses the half note as its pulse.

Diatonic: The collection of pitches that belong to the natural major or minor set of a key's scale or key signature.

Double Barline: Two lines placed next to one another (usually at the end of a piece) signifying the conclusion of a phrase, movement, or selection.

Dynamic: The value assigned to a note that determines its volume.

Eighth Note: A note half the value of a quarter note and twice the value of a sixteenth note.

Embouchure: The manner in which the mouth is positioned on an instrument.

Fermata: A symbol indicating that the player is to hold a note longer than written.

Grace Note: A smaller note attached to a larger note that is meant to be played right before the main note it is attached to. Grace notes can be played before or on a beat, depending on whether they are slashed. Slashed grace notes are played before the beat and un-slashed grace notes are played on the beat.

Half-hole: The act of covering half the hole of an instrument to create a semitone or microtone (a rare note smaller than a semitone).

Half Note: A note that is played for half the duration of a whole note and twice the duration of a quarter note.

Interval: The distance between two notes and/or two notes played at the same time.

Key: The collection of pitches that create the diatonic set for a base note.

Key Signature: The indication at the beginning or middle of a piece that shows which key is to be played or, at the very least, which set of pitches are considered default.

Ledger Line: Lines added above or below a staff to extend the written range of an instrument's part.

Measure: The section of a piece of music that encompasses the space between two barlines on a staff. Almost exclusively, a measure contains the total number of beats suggested in the time signature.

Meter: The rhythmic value of a selection of music; whether is it divisible by two or three.

Metronome: Musical device used to keep a steady pulse of time.

Mouthpiece: The part of a wind or brass instrument that is inserted into the mouth.

Note: A pitch and duration of sound indicated by a symbol in music.

Notate: The writing of notes.

Octave: A series of eight notes occupying the interval between (and including) two notes, one having twice or half the frequency of vibration of the other. This means the notes are directly proportionate to one another, the same way 1, 10, and 100 are directly proportionate to one another.

Pickup Measure: A measure, usually in the beginning of a piece, that is shorter than what is suggested by the key signature.

Pitch: The value of how high or low a note is.

Quarter Note: A note that is played twice as long as an eighth note and half as long as a half note.

Register: The set of pitches in the range of instrument(s) or selection(s).

Repeat Sign: Notated bar symbol signifying the repetition of a section.

Repertoire: A collection of works for a given instrument or group of instruments.

Rest: A period of suggested silence in a piece of music.

Ritard: Notated as *"rit."*, it signifies the slowing down of a passage, usually at the end of a piece.

Scale: Any set of notes arranged in ascending or descending order, usually with a consistent pattern of whole tones and semitones.

Semitone: Half of a whole tone; the smallest (diatonic) interval in western music.

Sixteenth Note: A note half the value of an eighth note and a quarter of the value of a quarter note.

Slur: The suggestion of performing a line or melody with no interruption of airflow or sound.

Staff: The set of five horizontal lines and four spaces that each represent a different musical pitch or, in the case of a percussion staff, different percussion instruments.

Step: An interval spanning no more than a whole tone.

Tie: Similar in appearance to the slur, but with the functionality of combining the lengths of the notes tied.

Timbre: The quality of the sound produced by an instrument.

Time Signature: The indication of a beat source and the amount of beats each measure is intended to have.

Tongue: To gently or firmly separate notes by interrupting airflow with the tongue.

Treble Clef: The most common clef, the symbol placed at the beginning or middle of a piece or selection indicating the location of *G* on its staff.

Triplet: The division of a beat or group of beats into three.

Tuning: The alteration of a pitch to match a desired frequency value.

Whole Note: A note twice the value of a half note and four times the value of a quarter note.

Whole tone: The distance of two semitones.

Woodwind: Any instrument that uses air that is not a keyboard or brass instrument.

If you've enjoyed reading this book, subscribe* to my mailing list for exclusive content and sneak peeks of my future books.

Visit the link below:

http://eepurl.com/duJ-yf

OR

Use the QR Code:

(*Must be 13 years or older to subscribe)

Made in United States
Orlando, FL
08 November 2022

24334295R00059